I KNOW IT ISN'T FUNNY
BUT I LOVE TO MAKE YOU LAUGH

OTHER BOOKS BY RIC MASTEN

R I C   M A S T E N
Artwork-Reed Farrington

i know
it isn't funny but...
i love to make you laugh

Revised Edition; including
the Walt Whitman Extension

SUNFLOWER INK - 37931 PALO COLORADO, CARMEL, CA 93923

The poems included in *the Walt Whitman Extension*
are all new and unpublished.
The poems in I KNOW IT ISN' T FUNNY BUT...
are largely reprinted from the following
out-of-print books:
Looking for Georgia O'Keeffe,
They Are All Gone Now and So Are You,
the Deserted Rooster,
Dragonflies, Codfish & Frogs,
all published by Sunflower Ink.

PRODUCED BY
NICHOLS & DIMES
2700 Country Club,
Odessa, Texas 79762
Telephone (915) 367-3562

I KNOW IT ISN'T FUNNY BUT...
I LOVE TO MAKE YOU LAUGH
Revised Edition; including
The Walt Whitman Extension

98765432

ISBN 0-931104-41-6
Library of Congress
Catalog Card Number: 95-092722

iv

DEDICATION

To the memory
of my stepfather, Dr. Chester W. Hare
and my aunt, Eleanor Taylor James

CONTENTS

FOREWORD

Good-humored people who smile as they talk are sneaky – we tend not to think of them as revolutionaries and radicals even when they are. Ric Masten is one example. What he says is penetrating and, sometimes, painful. The way he says it is disarming. You have heard that the best professionals "make the difficult look easy." Ric has accomplished this on two levels: he makes difficult writing look easy to do, and he makes difficult truths easy – or at least easier – to accept. And he does it by smiling through his writing.

Alas, some people think smiling is a limitation. Most of our important cultural landmarks have an air of grimness about them. Rodin's Thinker broods. Picasso's blue period is his most expensive. Faulkner's characters stumble to their dooms in Southern fogs. Hamlet, the melancholy Dane, moodily wanders the frigid halls of Elsinore. And in music – now don't peek – beetled-browed Beethoven rails and rages at the world.

I have always harbored a secret grudge against a culture that honors these grim gods so narrowly. The gods I honor and read, when I am not trying aggressively to make cultural points, when I'm just reading to learn about life and enjoy myself a bit in the process, are seldom mentioned with the Faulkners: S.J. Perelman, (I have a whole shelf of him), Max Beerbohm, Robert Benchley ... and Ric Masten.

Ric tackles topics as near to my soul as his brothers grim, but his approach is different. Instead of unloading a mountain on our heads, he is willing to sample truth, to bring back a pebble from the moon and let us admire, think and wonder. The fact that it is a pebble makes it easier to see. And he talks in a quiet voice – the better to hear him with.

So Ric is helping to disperse the cultural gloom a bit, and he is not alone. One of our most serious professions – medicine – has recently discovered laughter. Norman Cousins, Joseph Heller, and Dr. Bernie Siegel, among others, have all written that laughter is important in combating sickness. Alas, lawyers are still holding out. There are jokes about them, but very few by them. Ric – do you do missionary work? I have an assignment....

Jim Parkman
Hermosa Beach, California.

i know
it isn't funny but...
i love to make you laugh

personals

Official Portrait

i look so on top of it –
brow arched slightly – eyes alive with good humor
jaw set and yet around the mouth the hint of a smile
all of the above below the illusion of a pile of hair
but damn – it bothers me to see that face of mine
so full of confidence
gazing out into the not too distant future
which is where i am today
doing my best to recall that place in time

it was taken on request that much i know
and in a studio so i'm sure the thing was posed
clothes carefully chosen – head tipped just so
hair mussed as if by the wind – lips moistened
posture and expression set absolutely right
but like a suspicious dollar bill
i hold my glossy image to the light
but still i cannot say if what i see was real or not
but if it was then i fear the hooded photographer
took more than my photograph that day

better to be caught with my finger in my nose
mouth wide open – eyes drooping closed
with a tree that seems to be growing from my ear
appearing like an idiot and yet surrounded
by those who could love me still
if you must take my photograph
wait!... till after the curtain calls are done
and catch me falling off the stage
into the big bass drum

By Any Other Name

most of us
it would seem
are trying to live up to
or struggling to rise above
the momentary whimsy
of our parents

and what could mine have been thinking of
calling me Ricky?
Rickys never amount to anything
Hamiltons
address joint sessions of Congress
Sterlings race Maseratis
but Ricky?
hell
it's lucky i didn't grow up to be
a German Shepherd

and i've recently noted
that the Ricks
who drop the k for theatrical reasons
have become the groundlings
of the movie industry
never credited as writer
director or star
bestboy and gaffer is what the Rics are
boomman and grip
shunned
by women of mystery and elegance
Ric goes home with Patty or Babs

4

oh to have been christened
Wallace or Gregory
taken seriously
by editors of literary quarterlies
the Sidneys and Sheldons
who never venture beyond my name
convinced
that anything composed by a Ric
would have to be Mother's Day drivel
or doggerel for girlie magazines

desperate
i toy with the idea of running
first and last name together
ignoring the space as children often do
becoming Ricmasten
taking the lotus position
like Krishnamurti
venerated at last
but impossible
to find in the phone book

On the Tragic Death
of My Little Self

i was one
who clung grimly to childhood
still playing with toy soldiers
at thirteen

my favorite
a tiny cast-iron pirate
ruled the shelf
thumbs thrust in a wide belt
legs spread defiantly
scuffed and scarred
from a lifetime of adventure
he was my alter ego
and i called him My Little Self

together we lived through
the seven-year BB Gun Wars
trials by fire
mud slides ... cave-ins
unscathed we walked away
from countless tree-fort free-falls
diving to the depths of Mr. Near's lily pond
we stalked the golden killer whale

and once
the Southern Pacific thundered
by as we stood unflinching
between the clamoring rails
yes My Little Self and i
had survived it all

then one fateful day
fastened securely
to a length of twine
i flushed him down the toilet
and while winding him back to safety
the lifeline broke and he was gone
swept away
in one great resounding rush

oh
the irreversible
unfairness of it all! i wept ...
rending my clothes... tearing my hair
refusing to open the bathroom door
till my frightened parents
promised to buy me a new recruit
but it was Sunday
the stores were closed tight

and by Monday it was too late
puberty had arrived
and that brazen
invincible spirit of mine
was lost forever
in a maze of subterranean pipe

An Exercise in Caring

remaining close
to a chronic case of halitosis
must certainly be a measure of one's love
during lengthy dissertations
to stand unflinchingly at ground zero
is this not the stuff
heroes are made of?

it takes real dedication
to have intimate conversations
with someone whose fierce exhaust
can foul a gymnasium
and to do it in a Volkswagen bug

when we are together
the breeze always comes
from the direction of the dump
"something must be terribly wrong
 with the pump at the sanitation plant!"
yet i staunchly remain faithful
after each hug
holding my breath out the door

it takes more than a little affection
to be friends with a talking stockyard
to always be there when needed
and at the same time be upwind

god knows
i've tried to clear the air between us

dropping Dentyne hints
or more subtly calling your attention
to all the creativity it takes
to make an effective Listerine ad
to say nothing about the fortune
squandered on your behalf
carloads of Certs purchased
and sprinkled in your path
placed strategically on car seats
in coat pockets and all to no avail

it's obvious
i should simply sit you down
and give it to you straight
but when
it comes to finding the nerve to do this
i always find i fail

a poem
an ode to an anonymous friend
is the best that I can do
and if you come away from reading this
unrecognized and unaware
then i guess you'll never know
you have breath that curdles air

as for me
an ill wind calls my bluff
no matter how much i say i care
i've never cared enough

Hildreth

Mother...
if i were God in Heaven
who would you send to spend eternity with me?

the cherub
in the photograph
crying – holding a doll by the foot

the tomboy
racing a motorcycle
golden hair flying

the flapper
smoking her cigarette
in a long ivory holder

the perfect mother
parading a line
of perfect children

the widow
lifting her veil
married again in four months

the globetrotter
home with souvenirs
and an addiction

the alcoholic
the recovering
alcoholic

the eccentric
trying to look Egyptian
but resembling
a Buick hood ornament

the closeted recluse
watching Wimbledon
from a queen-size bed

and now
a timid old woman
all nose and chin

Mother...
here on the eve of your departure
i don't know who to put on the elevator

i only know that after some debate
your sons
will send your ashes east
to Massachusetts
where you have always said
you wanted them to go

that is
until yesterday
when it was too late
to let you change your mind

Mother's Voice
as Part of the Estate

thank god
it wasn't me she doted on
otherwise i'd have been the one
chosen to inherit Birdy
mother's irksome parrot
that dubious honor was bequeathed
to her youngest son... the pet...
the one who could always get
his way with the queen...
got it in the end...
the talking albatross i mean

the rest of us stifling a grin
as we watched the two of them begin
an ephemeral relationship
that didn't make it through the fall
but then
i doubt if anyone could live
with the disembodied voice
of a dear departed mom
still calling his name
"Donn!"
still ruling the roost
cigarette hack and all

my daughter Jerri
the Florence Nightingale
of animal husbandry
was next in line to take the orphan in
and climb the wall...

12

mother's prattling remains
quickly passed along
to an unsuspecting friend
who out of desperation
took the bird
to see a pet psychiatrist
and the fowl lobotomy that followed
exorcised out every vestige
of mother's zany sense of humor
leaving Birdy
well-behaved but spiritless
enunciating
with the generic inflection
of a network radio nonentity

and now that it's over
i kick myself in the pants
for not seizing the opportunity
to tape-record our family history
while i still had the chance

You Can't Win for Losing

"you can't win for losing"
is a time-worn phrase
by definition an aphorism
however such a lightweight
frivolous sounding term
hardly describes the last real conversation
i had with my stepbrother Jimmy

i was just back from studying art in Paris
he from a tour of duty in Korea
loosened by drink our homecoming reunion
had slipped to the place
where one would have thought
it was safe to praise the dead

"Jimmy" i said
"i hope you realize
 what a remarkable man your father was...
 in all the years he stood in as my dad
 never once did he make me feel that i
 his stepson
 was less important to him than you"

"that's quite true" said Jim
getting up to go
and going for good i might add
"never once in all those years did my real dad
 ever say or do
 anything to make me feel
 that i might have been a bit
 more important to him than you"

14

Pitfall

at wit's end
we persuade our errant son to join us
for fifty minutes with Ron Cobley
therapist and long time friend
which he did – bursting into the session
like a third-world terrorist
lips on automatic – firing from the hip

"if i'm screwed up
 it's my egomaniac father's fault
 consumed in a writing career
 he assiduously ignored the family
 my three sisters winding up
 a hypochondriac – a hard-line Marxist –
 and an air-head fashion plate
 Mom pickled in the cooking sherry turned sour
 giving good ol' Dad an excuse to crawl into bed
 with his little Orphan Annie fan
 Mother immediately retaliating tit for tat
 of course as is well known
 they managed to navigate
 the middle-age crazies by going public
 every intimate personal detail spread out
 and published in that stupid self-help
 psycho-babble pop-psychology book"
then to the therapist...
"a book which YOU read!"

slicking his hair down
he heads for the door smugly blowing smoke
off the end of an index finger

The Spanish Artist

because
my daughter taught
at the Institute of International Studies
the Spanish artist
did not come as a big surprise...
that he would suddenly pack her
and the new-born baby off
to live forever in Barcelona was

as was
the bleak realization that aside
from some peeks through Polaroid eyes
that baby is gone forever
oh there will be visits
later on
where this shy foreign little girl
is pushed forward
to kiss the cheeks of strangers...
a foot taller at each appearance
embarrassed by all the fuss
then in her teens
horrified by what the intervening years
have done to us

time is friendlier
when it passes from day to day

up until now
i've never given a thought
to my European forebearers

left behind
waving a hat from the end of the pier
over here in America
Odysseus is where it's at
who cares about Penelope
it is only important that she be there
to see you off and wish you well
resisting the temptation
to tell a Spanish artist
to go to hell!

Conversation

i have just wandered back
into our conversation
and find that you are still rattling on
about something or other
i think i must have been gone at least
twenty minutes
and you never missed me

now this might say something
about my acting ability
or it might say something about
your sensitivity

one thing troubles me though
when it is my turn to rattle on for twenty minutes
which i have been known to do
have you been missing too?

Mickey Rooney
& Judy Garland

with a kind of early Mickey Rooney
Judy Garland innocence we go before the church
and state exchanging unspoken trust
for legal documents the sole intent of which
is meant to cover and protect
all moonstruck lovers from themselves
when later in the course of human events
comes the expected divorce and property settlement

the magic and excitement traded off
for false security – signed – sealed
and written down – the guarantee
that neither he nor she will ever screw around

and didn't we go down beneath the weight
of this iron bouquet
dead
preserved in the state of wed-LOCK
and is it any wonder that pickled in this
atmosphere
the act of love becomes a habit
like eating in a Chinese restaurant
only because it's close and handy
sitting down together with the empty sound
of clicking silverware and nothing left between
but pork chow mein and strained silence
the bill always coming
with fortune cookie wisdom
like
"he who catches bus

will never have to chase it"
and other sad commentaries
written by some poor sap and his wife
trapped forever in a cookie factory
on the outskirts of every city and town
in America

The Chicago Fire

No one knows what goes on be-
hind the faces, for I live in your
golden shadow blinded by a rush of
bright madness, of burning morning
haze, and it is a wonder that I func-
tion at all.

Yet here in Virginia I wander
down this quiet afternoon with
friends and clearly see the dogwood
exploding in a galaxy of gray turn-
ing green. At my feet tiny flowers,
fern and moss are seen in perfect de-
tail.

Far from the midwest we walk at
the edge of spring, talking lightly of
things, voices in the trees, and no
one knows that i am being consumed
by the thought of you.

but now
in another space
another place and time
i read the above curiously
like an old newspaper account
of the Chicago fire
having no idea
of what it's really all about

like pain
such things
will not be remembered

The Quality of Love

in the throes of the affair
i was surprised to learn
i could love two women with intensity
at the same time
one with whom i'd spent many years
and one recently met

now
the quality of these loves
is best described by the difference
in my bathroom behavior – toilet procedure
at home – though the room was occupied
(my wife in the tub)
when ya gotta go ya gotta go
and i always went
but in an apartment near Chicago
i would carefully close the door
run the water and turn the fan on

during this time
if a doctor had informed me
i had but six months to live
looking back
i think i would have chosen the apartment
for the first three months
but i know now
i would have wished to go home to die
with someone who knows
just how full of crap
i really am

22

Woman
on the Eve of Emancipation

it was one of those off the wall
three o'clock in the morning
zap you wide awake
telephone calls

"do you think i have it in me
  to pack up the kids... climb in the car...
  cross the entire nation
  and start a new life in the east?
  i mean completely release myself
  from the stifling situation that has me trapped...
  putting it behind me for good?

  well today
  that's exactly what's happening...
  today is the day i drive away
  from this crummy neighborhood...
  split from this backward city and state
  mostly of course
  extract myself from territory
  infected by the cheap chauvinist centerpiece
  of the worst marriage i ever had
  and the mere anticipation
  of never seeing the louse again
  won't let me sleep"

"okay then
  why don't you get up and get going now"
i enthused
"i can't... i've still got to clean the house"

Birth Myth

one of my earliest memories
is that of my mother
holding forth
with the story of my birth

"talk about hard labor
how about 42 hours' worth ...
Doctor Hugh
hauling on the forceps
like a frontier dentist
and pain so intense
i doubt if even the most dedicated
masochist could bear it
Ricky's silly little elongated head
appearing at last
all red and resembling a carrot
honestly
when i saw how pointed he was
i went into hysterics
guffawing till stitches burst
and had to be re-sewn
i mean
i really thought the nurse
had brought an ice-cream cone"

god
how i resented being grist
for mother's sense-of-humor mill
remaining pissed until my own children
made me face the fact

that for all intents and purposes
i have taken the same act
on the road

it's time
to stop mining the mother load
to quit whining
and go to her defense
and say on her behalf
that...
"she knew it wasn't funny
 but she loved to make you laugh"

the view
from a slightly
jaundiced i

The View
from a Slightly Jaundiced I

until digested
what we put into our stomachs
is still
on the outside of us

male/female
young/old
it matters not

each of us
is simply an object
with a hole through it

stretch the imagination
and people
are really shaped like inner tubes
doughnuts and bagels
gentiles and jews

A Place for Conservatives

i must admit it bothers me more
than just a little bit
to see an airline pilot with dandruff
sitting around slightly wrinkled
chewing gum looking like any one of us
i mean
when you see the crew
go passing through the gate
don't you want the captain to be
a tight-lipped man
with close-cropped hair
eyes like steel doors slammed shut
crisp white shirt
slacks creased so sharply
if you weren't careful
you could get a nasty cut there

why i'd turn in my boarding pass
just like that
if some freaky long-haired cat
came bopping by
with an earring on one side
saying
"hey baby
  i'm gonna take us for a ride"

believe me i'm finally convinced
there really is a place for conservatives
or would you go to a neurosurgeon
who bit his fingernails?

30

seen knocking his drink over all the time
i mean
would you really want to do business
with either one of these guys
the morning after
he fought all night with his wife?
not on your life
not me at least
if i'm getting on that plane
going under that knife

what we need here
are hard minded
cold blooded
machine-like people
in a culture as techno-
logically advanced as ours has become
we cannot all afford to be
human

The Divine Wind

human nature being what it is...
the military arsenal
being what it has become...
questions arise

backed into the same desperate corner
would a Napoleonic paperhanger
commit suicide these days?
or apocalypse?

pushed to the brink
do you think a godless dirty commie
would surrender unconditionally
to a capitalist pig? – or vice versa?

the fact is
an atheist might be less inclined
to blow up the here and now
than those among us who believe
in a sweet by-and-by...
there is no defense
against a Kamikaze fundamentalist
willing to die flying prophecy
down the smokestack of human existence

even so
the heavyweights pose and bristle
confident as battleships
while dissidents on both sides
are ordered to get their thinking straight

A Negative Peace

out of the tenderloin
the madman came
a length of twine trailing from one hand
doing the breast stroke with the other
"clear the way!
 clear the way!
 here comes my submarine!"

the crowd separated
and spread-eagled against the buildings
one by one they sank into the stone
"submarine! submarine!
 step aside for my submarine!"

cars skidded and turned over
traffic snarled
and when he saw i wasn't buying it
he screamed
"look out!
 radioactive war machine!"

right here the question surfaces...
should i back off and give him more reason
to believe he has what he thinks he has
on the end of that string?

or should i stubbornly stand my ground
refusing to budge
and risk getting myself
run down by the damn thing?

Buel

Buel
i've seen the eyes lookin'
at my beard in the Mississippi airport
i've seen prejudice – hell
i've hid in the men's room – two hours
waiting for my plane – just showin' my feet
i've seen prejudice – but you're right
i can shave it off
i'll never see those eyes
lookin' out from inside black skin

Buel
have you ever seen a honky
and felt anything but anger – maybe envy?
have you ever looked at your black brother
and felt anything but pride – maybe shame?
how about guilt
you ever felt that lookin' at me?
i do lookin' at you
not because
my people did your people over
my people also worked kids to death
in the work house
fed Christians to lions...
burned witches too
but that was my people – not me
and i ain't gonna hang in my family tree

i'm only guilty
of being unable to ignore

34

the color of your skin
like i was taught i was supposed to do
when i was a kid and there isn't any way
you could know about this
being black
or for me to tell you being white

but Buel
i been lonely
can you understand that?

When Giants Pass

me in 1963: "Martin Luther King?
 isn't he the guy they keep putting in jail
 for disturbing the peace?"
from here somehow
by a route too circuitous to detail
i come around in the close dusky atmosphere
of Bethel Baptist Church
abruptly aware of surroundings
minus the glare of light off white skin
feeling conspicuous – unable to conform
i bob on the surface
of the dark moist murmuring warm

what the visiting preacher
said there that evening remains a blur
yet i vividly recall the shoe
being on the other foot
and exactly
where in that packed assembly hall
the two other white faces were

afterward
at the reception
i observe the guest of honor
being shyly avoided
no one goes near him at all
he stands alone
looking tired and incredibly small
so i go up to the man
and in a well meaning

36

good natured show business way
clap him on the back
and say
"working you pretty hard are they?"

i still can't believe
i said that to Martin Luther King
and neither could he
looking up sharply
at such a blatant display of naivete
then with patience and remarkable grace
said simply
"yes – but it's worth it"

i tell this story
in much the same way
Jubal George Taylor
my grandfather on my mother's side
described the day
when as a small boy
he stood with others by the railroad tracks
in a dismal grey rain
"i didn't know it then" he would say
"but i saw
  Abraham Lincoln's funeral train"

Michelangelo

high in the scaffolding on his back
Michelangelo bites his lip – sighs
and then begins to paint the hand of God
down

below
sweeping the chapel floor
a little serf leans his broom against the wall
squints up
and with an armful of trash stumbles out through a
graceful arch mumbling to himself

damn faggots

The Second Coming

go!
tell the Catholics
tell the Protestants
the Millennium is here!
at long last
God has acknowledged
two thousand years
of prayers prayed

Jesus has reappeared
in all his glory!

i know
because i saw him
at the Hospice
tenderly washing the feet
of a man who was dying
of AIDS

He Being Hefty
and She Full Figured

Don Rickles' sense of humor
would seem mean and vicious
coming out of Robert Redford
so
i hope i'm bald enough
and funny enough looking
in a bathing suit
to get away
with telling you about
what came to mind
during the tender performance
of a love song
composed and rendered
by a fat man
for his even fatter fiance

a seaside song
a two silhouettes
walking the silver strand
hand-in-hand type song
windswept
with salty kisses
and ocean spray
a beautiful day in a love-
life song
but
when you know
you're not supposed to think
about whales

40

whales
are all you can think about

beached whales
frolicking in the surf
the scene
in *From Here To Eternity*
played out
on an immense corpulent scale
tons of fun heaped
on a wet slippery rock
collapsing the dock
acres and acres of sunburn
and footprints two feet deep

caught
in the undertow
swept along on a riptide
of uncontrollable thought
i almost miss
what is most important here
set to music – in song
all of us appear
ageless attractive and trim
able to see each other
as he saw her and she saw him

Adventures
in the Nasal Passage

at even
the slightest suggestion
of a bird in the mailbox
peeking out
interpersonal communication
takes a real nose dive

faced with this distracting situation
victory over death
a sure-fire get-rich-quick plan
erotic dissertations on sex
no topic
can override my desire
to conjure up a box of Kleenex...
a handkerchief...
a shirtcuff for god's sake!

where are the public relations
people when we need them?

if this much-maligned object
could somehow be imbued
with an air of glamor
a sighting might become
a positive experience
not something
to turn away from in disgust

this having been accomplished
no doubt
societies would quickly form
and like
the Audubon go on field trips...
every novice
eager to spot a barn owl
"the trick Mildred
  is in knowing where to look"

enthusing like rockhounds
"wow!
  look at the beauty Jack found!"

like wild flowers the prizes picked
and pressed between the pages
of leather-bound books...
valuable human achievements
not unlike tears

and in recognizing this
we take another tentative step
away from
an incapacitating prejudice...
able
to lunch with Quasimodo
without a second thought

The First Lady

on a popular television game show
a man and woman co-host
they appear together
while he runs down the list of prizes

the exciting self-supporting
medium-duty jib crane
with pillar-base mounting!

for problem-free paper sticking!
a year's supply of Carter's
non-wrinkling
waterproof rubber cement

and of course the biggie!

the all-expense-paid
weekend vacation
on the island of Guam!

as always
trying to make something
out of nothing
i study the face of the female
on camera
but not speaking
the enthusiastic listener
who eagerly nods over each item
emitting testimonial sounds
from a tiny round mouth
ooh! ah! oh!

44

cringing
i wonder what it would take
to have me
standing at someone's elbow like that
animated
with my arms dangling

the audience loving me for it

Old Oraibi
and the Videophone

imagine looking into the eyes
of the voice speaking in your ear
putting substance with sound
imagine the improvement
in interpersonal communication

when a poet speaks near Old Oraibi
the Native Americans
hear everything that is said
while watching the ceiling and floor

"never the face
  it would be a display of great disrespect
  to intrude in such a private place
  we only stare at those
  who are not quite human beings
  for furniture salesmen
  and government agents
  we have a saying:
  do not step sideways too quickly
  white-eyes
  or you will surely disappear"

as she spoke the Hopi woman smiled
studying the sky

elsewhere
the advent of the videophone
will turn out to be little more
than a boon for flashers

46

The Good Feeling
of Leaving a Room Knowing
You're Not Missing Anything

suppose all the crap on TV
vanished miraculously
leaving on tap
a full schedule of quality programing...
"how wonderful!" you say
well i say: "be careful!"
if television ever got as good
as i would like it to get
i've seen my last live sunset

of course
presented with a complete lineup
of unending excellence
the existing population of couch potatoes
would come pouring forth
fleeing from the clutches of *Masterpiece Theater*
and the *MacNeil-Lehrer Report*

legions of sit-com
soap and game show fanatics
unearthed and shambling around
like creatures from *Night of the Living Dead*
arms extended – staring straight ahead
today's major market share
stunned and bewildered
by the awful burden that accompanies freedom

when it comes to good taste
and television fare
i say pray for a wasteland

Garden Club Existentialism

unable to get going today i allowed myself
time to lie around the house fallow
watching afternoon TV
and my god
i had no idea how awful life could be

—you see there was this young lab technician who
wanted to marry a blind girl not because he loved
her which he didn't but because he had fathered her
first child when she'd been married to his alcoholic
brother

—the brother in the meantime had developed lung
cancer while in prison, but the surgeon who was to
perform the operation had been murdered by the
blind girl's mother who had gone mad after being
bitten by a tropical insect that was part of the young
lab technician's experiments

—all this happened when the mother tampered
with these experiments hoping to discredit him so
that her daughter might remarry the alcoholic
brother who had quit drinking and what with the
operation and everything needed all the help he
could get ...

and i sat there dumbfounded
through a soap commercial and the preview
of tomorrow's *Ongoing Agony*
after which i got up

and went into the bathroom
with a wrench
and in two minutes repaired a faucet
that had been leaking for a year and a half
then
resting on the edge of the tub admiring
my handiwork i laughed till i cried

which all goes to prove
that there ain't no such thing as a happy
ending but if you're willing to settle for less
you can have some real good times
along the way

the time squeeze

The Time Squeeze

the time squeeze
is a science fiction film
in which John Wayne and Bette Davis
are contemporaries
but the casting
director has kept them apart

for John
the leading lady
must be freshened like a drink
a testimonial female...
a dream inflated with youth
and though he might act differently
she always leaves him exhausted
after a love scene
with no one to talk to
except the ghastly remains
of Ward Bond and Gabby Hayes

and Bette
didn't always cackle that way
forced to play a crazy old crone
once she too
had muscle tone and defied gravity
but when a woman's face
has been lived in
long enough to have something to say
who would listen
so she makes it up each morning

like a bed
and pays a surgeon to hide the scars

bored with this
the Pepsi generation
is out in the lobby buying popcorn
to them it was just another foreign film
they could read the subtitles
but couldn't understand what they were seeing

and
even i
laughed and cried in all the wrong places
till the houselights came up
and i could see the back of my own hands

Toto Something Tells Me
This Ain't Kansas...

"and the dogs dwindle down
to a precious few...
September..."

the seven-to-one theory
makes our old dog Grace
a hundred and twenty-six
she arrived on my birthday
fun fixed up in a ribbon
i was thirty-five and we went for a run

and now on my fifty-third
i'm puppied again
this time though
no spontaneous jog
just me
looking from dog to dog
calculating
that when he is as old as she...
my god i'm seventy!

i know
age is a state of mind – a point of view
and i don't mean to be depressing
but figured in terrier time
i'm already three hundred and seventy-two

and that, Dorothy
is far enough over the rainbow
to know
i haven't got many more Totos to go

Coming of Age

i will admit
the young waitress
did flirt outrageously

my guess is
i closely resemble her dad
or perhaps her uncle Sid
the one who is such a big tease

but animal magnetism?
pleeese!

give it up boys
cut the hot-cha-cha
elbow in the ribs
i have a mirror
and a clear sense of myself

oh...
if i could wound her with a poem
show her moments
when i've held an audience
trembling in my grip
then perhaps

then
i might be something other
than the "balding little fat guy
who left an enormous tip"

Sleep

sleep...
recently i have been going to you
as an old fool to a secret lover
and not unlike a tired salesman
bored with his territory
i have been giving in to temptation
sneaking off in the afternoon
for a quickie little nap
a diversion
always coming out of it with a start
a twinge of fear
telling myself
i shouldn't be here like this with you

but late in the evening
when the time is right
and what we do together is socially acceptable
shamelessly
i can give myself to you completely
forgetting the past
letting the future go
and oh
how i hate to leave you in the morning

sleep...
you have become an acceptable death
lovers of life – a warning

The Peter Pan Syndrome

Michael
the jeans no longer fit
i have taken to wearing trousers
this
while you run with a crowd
younger than our children
having food fights

Diet Pepsi and aerobics...
belly flat as a plank of walnut
reminding me of a time
when i myself tried to beat the devil
winding up "with an old man's head
on a young man's body"
she laughingly said

and yet here you are
armed with a sympathetic ex-wife
racing a Mercedes through the smoking ruins
of gutted love affairs
thriving on pain like an adolescent...
able to rake the most amazing poetry
from off the floor of this furnace

and Michael
except for the dark howl of your eyes
i am envious of everything
but recently
I have lost the desire
to drive around with the top down

58

or fry on a towel poolside
the dancing fool is no more
i pay for my mistakes
with Alka-Seltzer

this evening over dinner
i'll interpret our encounter for my wife
and like an accomplished jazz musician
improvise around the part
where in the sack later
i will be the one with the headache

however...
first thing tomorrow morning
i plan to visit a medical facility
and buttonhole a doctor
requesting
no ... demanding
that he find something wrong with me

The Business of Dying

in my twenties
i went along with Dylan Thomas
boasting
that i wanted to die
looking death squarely in the eye

thirty years later however
this brash statement
was somewhat revised...
nowadays
i find myself hoping it happens
like it happens
to the sentry keeping guard
in all those Fort Apache movies
found dead
face down an arrow in the back
" poor devil"
the Sergeant always said
"never knew what hit him"

i like that!

the end
taking me completely by surprise
the rest
left in the hands
of clever young writers
still wet behind the ears

The Handyman

it's autumn...
i feel it in my bones and other places

it's autumn...
i can no longer afford
to own a Cricket lighter
having thrown too much away already

it's autumn...
time to maintain
a not very exciting prospect
for those who remain in a springtime
summertime frame of mind
there is more to maintenance
than a drop of oil
a dab of glue
things gather value and interest
as you rub off the new

it's autumn...
and according to my wife
an old chest becomes a priceless antique
only
if it gets a good going over
at least twice a week

Ollie Williford

my bride came landscaped
with a multifarious forest of colorful relatives
so i really can't say her notorious grandmother
registered until
in the reception line
at our wedding
she got my full attention
with a big fat French kiss

"i'm your grandma Ollie!
  i've been married at least ten times...
  i'm gonna live to be a hundred
  and i won't be buried until i die!"

after that
i knew which one Ollie was
and carefully kept some distance
between myself and that amorous antique
that sexy old sneak
"over the hills and through the woods
  to grandmother's house we go"
took on new significance

in her sixties then
a bonafide sexagenarian
which i completely dismissed
as just another creaky coquette
rickety tease
another advanced case of hotpants

decades later
watching the *Today Show*
she survives
waiting for word from Willard Scott
(i wonder if Willard knows
 how many venerable vamps he keeps alive)

and she is alive!
on the edge of a second century
still with a roving eye
trillium pinned to her blouse
still with her arms reaching out
a living example of never-say-die
the original Granny Goose

and Ollie
while there's still time to tell you
i am seduced

A Quirk of Time

drifts
of flushed adolescents
checking out the ride and concession area...
in those days we eyed each other hotly

and then later
returned with children clamped to our legs
squeeling at the size of the prize pig

this August however
my dear sweet wife sits
in the middle of our bed weeping
because she no longer wants to go
to the Monterey County Fair
as much as she used to

and i
at the first sound of a Skilsaw
out planting a screen of trees
between us and the monstrosity going up
on the property adjoining ours
something i should have anticipated
and taken care of years ago
fast-growing eucalyptus and Monterey pine...
i figure fifteen years
before they do the job

i'll be in my seventies then

The Latest Wrinkle

the aging process proceeds
the latest wrinkle
being
that i can't go to the movies
the theater or anywhere else these days
without first
taking a little afternoon nap

without one
i am in grave danger
of paying hard-earned money
to spend an evening sleeping upright
in a room full of strangers

The Storm of '83

atmospheric upheaval
elements
wild enough to send Lear
back to his bolt-cloven tree
and mean enough
to close Highway 1 for a year

deluge...
pluvial downpour...
wet enough to give
a latter-day Noah ideas
and bring the choppers in low with Alpo
for the animals we left behind

oh
i suppose
in strictly scientific terms
it will be regarded
only
as an interesting moment
in meteorological history

but happening in my yard
in my lifetime
it was a disaster!
the kind of event
grandfathers have already
begun to exaggerate about

Upon Seeing a Digital Watch
for the First Time

if i live to be eighty
then i was more than halfway there
when Buzzy Jr.
flew his brand new Seiko
across the street

he
with the readout lit in liquid crystal
just a kid
and all that science on his wrist

me
mouth agape
with my pocket Ben twisting at the end of a chain
suddenly obsolete

it's like Grandville Glover
seeing an airplane for the first time
petrified
as the diving barnstormer
scattered the horses
and left the crowd screaming

the baffling moment
lodged irretrievably in his brain

Grandpa
pulling up lame
as the rest of the world
flew off in another direction

Mick Jagger Turns Eighty
and Talks About Old Times

i recall how old man Glover
would wait in the throat of family gatherings...
the slightest contact setting him off
like a Mackabe gopher trap

"hi Grampa"
was all it took to put me squirming on the hook
of the Great Depression
a young man learns
to sit at the far end of the table
and cut out early for a picture show

(In those days the feature attraction was always ac-
companied by short subjects. I remember one about
a scientist who went looking for himself in a time
machine. It ended with the boy he had once been,
on a park bench, beside the old man he was destined
to be. Unwilling to make the connection, they sat
there, back to back, like bookends while the credits
rolled.)

right here
i will have to admit
i'm not absolutely certain this film ever existed
a lot of what i remember didn't
but last Thanksgiving Day
while telling Walter my young nephew
about the hippies and what life was like
in the Haight Ashbury something
very definitely snapped shut

68

A Days of Yore Bore

i am worried
about the kind of old man i'm going to be
i fret
because i think i met him
twenty years ago in Pittsburgh
after a reading of my poetry

clearly his intent
was to simply pay a fellow author
a compliment
but the moment he had me by the hand
almost helplessly he began
beating his own drum
assaulting me with unbroken paradiddles
of past accomplishments

and if i hadn't been rude
cutting him off curtly i suspect
i'd still be in Pittsburgh
wiggling uncomfortably
tangled in the endless resume
of this aged Lilliputian

but then
looking at it from his point of view
a compliment doesn't mean much
when you don't know who it's from

"here
 let me give you one of my books"

in order to have an identity
some of us need
to be preceded by our deeds
ask me who i am
and i'll show you what i do
only recently coming to realize
that a day may come
when i'm too old to do it anymore
and god forbid
must introduce myself
by telling people what i did

"i don't mean to be a bore but..."

if ever
i get you by the ear
and won't let go – read this!
with each passing year
it becomes increasingly
more important for me to know
that you know
that i once knew
what's happening here

House of Grandfathers

in the house of grandfathers
the dusty old flowers sit around
fishing for smiles
sometimes they read stories to themselves
from torn yellow pages
and it is amusing for awhile
but they know why i come

it looks like hard work old man
and no one to lend a hand
except well meaning girls
coming like hornets with their stingers
getting in your way with cylinders
tubes and see-through tents

it seems to me if you were home
you'd be done with your labor
and resting already

i kept the watch awhile but couldn't stay

goodby old man – old dandelion
i wish i were the wind

"...and what is it
that you really do
for a living?"

A Poet?

being published
means something only
on the date of publication

had i known this
i would never have listed my occupation
as "poet"
when filling out forms
at the Credit Union

it would have been better
if i had described myself
as "voyeur"
or "manic-depressive"

i can see now
i should have slept on it...
accomplishments never seem to survive
a good night's sleep

the rejection slips however
the dead ends
are always there in the morning
like that bully kid
who gave me such a hard time
on the way to school

sneering...
asking me again today
"and what is it
  that you really do for a living?"

Cannibal

i see by the posters
you gave a reading at the forum last night
i didn't forget
i just didn't attend

had the meal tasted as good
as i suspected it would
foolishly i'd feel diminished
if undigestible – the evening wasted
either way i spared myself
what would have been
a miserable ordeal

if you have anything to do with poetry
i think you'll know and understand
how difficult it is
to go and watch someone else
serve up the eucharist...
to sit behind a hand and analyze the footwork
holding back petrified
that you'll get out of control
and eat it up
and enjoy it

a reformed cannibal
can't be too careful
so i keep myself away from any kind
of plump juicy missionary
and dine alone on my own
cold potatoes

76

See How Smoothly
His Jaw Moves

a tossed salad
lost in a field of tossed salads...
i try to distinguish myself
by describing the flavor of tarragon with gestures
i long to be experienced

like Langston Hughes i too have wilted
watching a house erode between
the potluck and poetry reading

"we'd love to stay
  but we really must go
  the ostriches you know..."

and it's just as indigestible
at the head table
where the fancy covered dishes congregate

"look out for this one Sidney
  it has liver in it..."

everyone sneaking a peek
to see what a poet looks like eating coleslaw
marveling
at how smoothly his jaw moves

staring straight ahead
i ask myself why just being at the table
has never been enough

Inventing the Wheel

i don't often read other poets
and i'll tell you why

when i finally get around
to sitting down in the middle of the road
to invent the wheel...
having spent days
gathering my materials around me
and having just figured out where to drill
the first hole
it's enough to make you break down and cry
to look up and see
some brilliant young S.O.B. on a bicycle
go pedaling by

A Very Serious Artist

when he wasn't teaching art
at the Community College
he was in his studio
making rocks out of store-bought clay

small stones
pebbles – pieces of gravel
buckets and buckets full
modeled after specimens
collected earlier in a previous life

no question about it
in a natural setting
his creations were convincing enough
to fool even an expert

rumor has it
he once lived somewhere
other than Odessa, Texas...
by the sea, they say
and with a woman

some of us it would seem
stubbornly try to recall feelings
when all we can really do
is remember we had them

For a Public Speaker
Is There Life after Death?

for Virginia Rose

"but Doctor
  how could you possibly
  have removed the wrong leg?"
i suppose
worse mistakes have been made...

nevertheless
mine was the kind of nightmare
one would give absolutely anything
to go to sleep from
and as you know Virginia
i wasn't there
so i can only surmise
what the program chair feels
fifteen minutes into the vacuum
and four hundred eyes on the door

somewhat akin i expect
to the panic that paralyzed my end
when putting the receiver to my ear
i heard your icy voice inquire
"why aren't you here?"

one thing i do know for sure
beyond excruciating and unbearable
levels of pain and shame
are indistinguishable

looking for ways to make amends
i have considered sending you

80

my life savings...
my first born child...
looking for absolution
i have called everyone i know
everyone except you Virginia
you
i could only face through the mail
and i do hope you took some satisfaction
from the detailed suicide note

as for the larger picture...
in the world news that very evening
it was reported that astronomers
in Australia
watched a star explode...
an extremely rare phenomenon
which
traveling at the speed of light
happened 150 thousand years ago

the prediction is
that the noticeable aftermath
left by this distant apocalypse
will dominate the night sky
down under
for centuries to come

and i do lie awake Virginia
wondering just what exactly
has been cut off here at the knee

Closet Poet
for Michael Forrest

i suspect you know precisely
how many poems fit in a cardboard box
perhaps even
the number of boxes it takes
before the furniture must go

who are you keeping these secrets for though?
yourself?
and/or that vague romantic notion you have
of being found up in a musty attic
some future kindred spirit
sitting on a dusty trunk
weeping over your mildewed remains

Emily Dickinson
was already at the cemetery
when Colonel Tom Higginson went to the closet
and discovered her collection of damask...
hand-sewn dreams
neatly folded away like fine linen

lucky for us
he and her inheritors were a determined
self-serving enterprising bunch

certainly everyone admires a shy private person
but be advised
without the pump of ambition
all the talent in the world
can come to no more than a couple of trips
to the dump

82

Damn You Gauguin
and All Other White Whales

for someone caught in the paper claw
of a corporate world
the watercolor hanging in his office
was good enough
to be terribly distracting

he had talent alright
enough
to keep one small part of his mind
waving free
like Ahab's arm
beckoning from that elusive dream

but how do you ask an orthodontist
to take the bands off the kid's teeth?
i mean
do you go to him and say
"remove the braces Dr. Bently
  i'm running off to the islands
  to be an artist
  and i can't afford them anymore"
or do you get a pair of pliers
and do it yourself?

the young and romantic
might find this hard to believe
but you simply cannot get to Tahiti from here

To a Literary Giant
and Other Daredevils

if i acted crazy – forgive me
but i'm a daredevil too
and when i arrived at the jump site
and saw the monstrous crowd pressing around you
i was afraid you might not see my bike

but you gave me a tired smile
and waved from the foot of the ramp...
a marvelous feat considering all the distractions

out on the edge a promise
is a dangerous contraption
having little to do with bravery

if you can't say "no"
your "yes" means nothing
and you are much too valuable
to waste on the Snake River

Another Kind of Noah

and yet
when my friend Marvin
the mad poet
comes out of the zoo every six months
one shoe on – one shoe off
i'm always glad to see he isn't cured
that he still limps in his mind – old nutty Marv
because you know i really don't want
to run the instant replay
of yesterday's baseball game
i need his insane rhymes
like straws to clutch at
not the box score – i watch him

Paul Gauguin
watching through his own window pain
his crazy friend Vincent
winding his head up in gauze
knowing the hurt to be the very ground
in which art grows
and far better for him at least
than filling galleries
with slick paintings of wet city streets
colors reflecting
or of little kids with big sad eyes
at fifty bucks a throw

and though it seems unfair of me
i need him there at sea – adrift
tending his mad menagerie

another kind of Noah
i need him there...
dropping me a line
each time i fall into that awful blue period of mine

even if i could have i would not have
spared Van Gogh the pain of cutting his ear off
and robbed myself of those sunflowers
sorry about that Vincent
sorry about that myself

and yet
for you who say be totally sensitive
know that i once knew a ditchdigger
who bled to death in his own trench
because he could not grow a callus...
couldn't play banjo either
without cutting himself to ribbons on the wires

i need my thick skin for protection
otherwise i couldn't say anything of consequence
without breaking down completely
right here in front of you
and you wouldn't want that now would you?
really...

total sensitivity
well...
it's sort of like an orgasm
you can only stand just so much of it
before you go right out of your gourd

86

A Moment of Truth

in some other life
i must have been a bullfighter
a little Spanish rooster...
hot stuff in my suit of lights
but not so hot on sleepless nights
my mind out there in the pens
where the bulls wait like mountains...
dark premonitions – milling around
restless – all my brave tomorrows

hey Amigo – tell me
is this where you really want to be?

no – not at all

except
in the afternoon
when there is no time to think
and hats are flying thick as crows

except
when i consider doing something
less dangerous for my sunflowers

except
when i parade through the kitchen
with a bleeding ear like this – held high
the fruit of the day – the prize!
and perhaps from you
a small "ole!"

Talkin' on the Talk Show
for Gary Tessler, KOA Denver

every Friday
at 11:45 Denver time
i, as a "regular feature of the show"
drop everything
and expose myself to millions...
an electronic flasher

lowering my voice
i try to project Orson Welles
reciting the Old Testament
but secretly suspect
it sounds more like Mickey Mouse
with nothing to say
"hi everybody!"

and how can i be certain
i'm not just standing in a closet
hearing voices ... talking to myself?

a hundred years ago
if i'd been caught doing this
they'd have put me away for sure
the orderlies exchanging glances
as i desperately try to explain
about having a Talk Show Host in my ear

nevertheless
every Friday at 11:45 Denver time
i duck into a telephone booth
and like Clark Kent

88

pray that this morning
i remembered to put on clean leotards

my god!
it's all so religious...
this casting bread upon the airwaves
and a true believer never doubts
the existence of a listening audience

he simply says his prayers
hangs up
and goes on about his business

Backstage

i am often taken in
by the stagecraft pictured
on the pages of *Sunset* magazine
settings
that speak to me somehow saying
"in this breakfast nook
  you will never be lonely again"

and i should know better
i who reside in a theatrical set
propped up on the apron
of the Santa Lucia mountains

from the road
everything looks real enough
but i know that the walls
are made of painted rags
and the tower
sways in the slightest breeze

on Sundays
they stream out from the city
passenger cars creeping by
people pointing
living for a moment in a poet's dream

i wave from the window
why not?
how could they know there's nothing
behind any of this

nothing except
what they bring to it themselves
this is not to say
that in this living space
there are not those rare moments
when we gather on the deck
to see a crescent moon at sunset
the air alive
with the sound of Rainbirds
whispering down in the garden

but
in the theatre
when the audience goes home
there is always that one
unblinking naked lightbulb left on
backstage

jock scraps

The Hypothetical Question

the hypothetical question
lies beside the road like a stone
and probably should be left entirely alone
it being hypothetical
should we bother with what we uncover
while turning it over?

suppose i should ask you
what you think you would do
if all other humans suddenly vanished...
leaving you
the last of mankind
and with the knowledge that you
are the absolute end of the line
everything else intact though
supermarkets – libraries
gas stations – animals
everything just as you'd find it today
minus people

alone
confronting this situation
do you think
you'd commit suicide then and there
without hesitation?
or do you think you couldn't do that
but most likely you'd wither away
going out of your mind in a very short time?
or are you someone who thinks
you could live your life out

combing beaches...
a dog at your side – a stick in your hand
like Robinson Crusoe
only this time with no hope
of finding Friday's prints in the sand
in short how much do you think you need
your fellow man?
well, ask a hypothetical question
get a hypothetical answer

or so i thought
till i was surprised
and brought down in flames
by a braless young girl...
a hard-line feminist who took aim and said

"boy...
 if i were the one
 in the problem you posed
 i would not commit suicide – comb beaches
 nor would i wither away
 those are the options
 of a male chauvinist pig!

 rather
 i would head for the nearest sperm bank
 and being a healthy female
 impregnate myself
 and start it all over again
 this time – thanks to science – minus men!"

like i said
the hypothetical question
lies beside the road like a stone
and probably should be left entirely alone
but turn it over
and usually the usual number
of salamanders – sowbugs
and centipedes will be uncovered

but look out
for an occasional black widow spider
who kills and devours her mate
a fact
that is not in the least bit hypothetical
and in a funny science fiction sort of way
food for thought

right fellas?

Circus Maximus

reaching for a mile she is
hoping for an inch she was
burning her bra
while the cameras pan the crooked smile
on the face of a nervous man
probably henpecked most of his life
the entire spectacle making good copy i guess
in the chauvinist press

but aside from the rhetoric and upraised fist
the central theme of the feminist
was best expressed in a speech
delivered from a double bed
when after twenty years of marriage
my wife said
"the economics of ERA
  will allow me to stay with you
  not because i have to but because
  and only because i want to"

this power play
more than any other has the gladiators
huddled beneath the Colosseum floor
clinging to the urinal in much the same way
early Christians clung to the cross
but in the words of one true believer
waiting to be flung to the lions...
"brother...
  you must admit
  these are sure exciting times!"

98

For Such a Brutal Primitive Sport
I Must Apologize

ladies
i hate to admit it
but there are times when i find
i haven't completely resigned
from the Neanderthal club
old Og
still needs a way to deal
with pent-up aggression
explaining perhaps
why the trip to the Super Bowl
has become such a national
obsession

but then
isn't it more humane and genteel
to tame the beast vicariously?
to sit
harmlessly watching a field
where padded paid professionals
hit and flog each other
isn't this better
than taking it out on the wife
the kids the dog and your mother?
to say nothing
about just possibly reducing
the risk of World War III

ladies i put it to you
isn't football really
the civilized thing to do?

Widows of the NFL

during the season
do not arrange social engagements
unless you have checked with him first
all dates are in doubt...
Sundays are sacred of course
but since Monday-night football
is now played on Thursday
rational thinking is out

and don't
try to circumvent this
by inviting friends over
to watch the game with your spouse
if they root for the other city
then the scene in the den will not be pretty
and probably end
with a swat team surrounding your house

however
if the cheering section is compatible
do plan to serve snacks during the action
not hor d'oeuvres – nothing fancy like that
just be sure to include something
from the five major food groups
caffeine – alcohol – sugar – salt and fat

and don't assume he's enjoying himself in there
rabid football fans are perpetually wretched
touchdowns ahead
they still feel defeated

convinced that they can't keep the lead
down by a point and it's hopeless
"we'll never score what we need!"

and it's really OK
for women to hate the game
better this than pretending to be a fan
a "sports buddy"
with a bright inquiring mind
trying to impress him with questions
about nickelbacks and pointspread
while he watches his team fall a field goal behind

but most of all
after the opening whistle has blown
don't get sexy
studies have shown
football renders the male impotent...
at game time cold showers are best
besides if you think about it
you have your own hands-off policy
during *Dynasty* and *Falcon Crest*

keep in mind though
the road to the Super Bowl
may seem endless
but a frustrated maid must not lose faith
as she lies alone in her bed
when the Pro Bowl is over
so is the season
and the couch potato will rise from the dead

The Annual Check-Up

every now and then
i discover this strange lump
in my abdomen which i finger
when no one is looking
to see if the soreness is still there
and it always is
and so in fear and trembling
i go to see my doctor
and hear the bad news
and this kindly old bird
hops around me
like a crow with a piece of tin foil
poking and peering
until stroking his chin
he declares
that i am in A-1 condition
and if i'd stop handling my pancreas
it wouldn't be so sore

and yet always in the end
i leave his office
with the certain knowledge
that i will be dead in six months
the good doctor
keeping my awful infirmities from me
so that i can enjoy
what little time i have left
and bravely with this information
hidden under my coat
i return home

to be with my family
and together
we climb the hill in back of the house
to sit a spell
and really watch a cloud move

i guess you'd say
i was a bit of a hypochondriac
and that's OK
it keeps me close to things
and on this ward we are all
terminal anyway

The Press
and the Presidential Polyp

suddenly the mind of America
focuses
on the place where the sun never shines

like characters
in a George Lukas movie
we are hurtled down a mile of twisting colon
light from the flexible sigmoidoscope
probing ahead
till rounding an undulating corner
i half expect to see Indiana Jones
leaning against an abnormal outcropping
a devil-may-care smile on his face

all the time
Dan Rather
like a Greyline tour guide
calling out points of interest
carefully explaining that the bowels
in which we were trespassing
were not actually the President's...
talk about an invasion of someone's privacy!

of course
for the delighted proctologist
it was all money in the bank
but for those of us who blanch
at the thought of a rubber glove
afraid to chance a medical check-up
for fear of what the doctor might find

believe me
these have been difficult times

i mean
if the Commander in Chief's villous adenoma
can go undetected
what hope do the rank and file have?

it would seem then
that an unrestrained press
has once again left the American public
en masse
with a quizzical finger up its collective...

Free at Last

if she's part of the movement
she no longer wants to be a girl
a chick
or a broad
not even a lady
she's a feminist
a liberated woman
and i'm for this
a free female
means a free male
free enough to openly express
my childish insecurity

if a person
wants to whine and whimper
nowadays a person can
but everytime i do
my liberated woman
says
"act like a man"

Prehistoric Residue

before we began eating bushes
the survival of the species really did depend
upon a man knowing exactly where the deer
and the antelope play
so i suggest that there are deep-rooted reasons
why i would drive around in circles forever
rather than stop and ask a native for directions
i mean
can you imagine the male ego
leaving itself that wide open to ridicule?

"pardon me sir but do you happen to know
  where the buffalo roam?"

"two blocks down and on your right wimp!
  and now i suppose you'll be wanting me
  to make the kill — skin it out
  and help you carry it home...."

permeated with such prehistoric residue
you'll never catch this closet macho man
shuffling up
to some know-it-all gas station attendant
my hat in my hand

after all
it takes thirty million sperm
to fertilize a single egg
Mother Nature knows the male entity
never stops to ask for directions

Travels
with the Wagon Master
and a Sanitary Engineer

i am a straightforward
goal-oriented
linear-type traveler
vacationing
like Patton racing for the Rhine

the unsmiling map-in-the-lap
mile-a-minute kind
in touch with where we are...
where we're going...
constantly
updating the arrival time

right on schedule
yet plagued
by the dreadful thought
that at any moment
my wife will wake from her nap
open her eyes
and see the road sign
that says
"Historical Marker 2 miles ahead"

and she
on the road
becomes a devout sanitarian
scouring the countryside
both figuratively
and literally

opening motel doors
with curled lip
and Lysol spray can going

"if you plan to sleep with me tonight
  keep your feet off this filthy floor!"

at bedtime
throwing back the covers
surveying the linen landscape
praying
that this time
there will be no sign
no historical marker
of another kind

Men Women & Maps

at sixty miles per
bearing down on one of those
infamous Cal Trans interchanges
i experience a rare moment
of directional doubt
"quickly!" i say to her
find out which route
bypasses downtown LA
to which
my nuptial navigator snaps
"don't shout"

then
handling our book of maps
like some strange alien object
she lets it fall open
on the state of North Dakota
where studious
as a bible scholar now...
with index finger extended
she actually starts to look

at this juncture
you will observe
the car swerve dangerously

of course
to hear her tell it
"after deciphering
  his garbled command

i instantly locate
the quadrant in question
efficiently analyze the situation
then in a voice calm and strong
brief the hysterical pilot
left on 5 – straight on
then left on 101"
to which she insists
i always respond...
"that has to be wrong!"

for couples
who travel the road of life
there are many twists and turns
but any mixture
of man woman and map
is always a can of worms

Changing Directions

as goal-oriented as a spear
the male has always given
travel instructions
in tenth-of-a-mile increments
complete
with an accurate stoplight count...
landmarks carefully indicated
along with the exact location
of every interstate
county road street and alley
with in five hundred miles
explaining
that a man likes to know
precisely where he is
and precisely how much farther
he has to go

more organic
a female will tell you
"to turn right
  where a tall rawboned woman
  is hanging the wash out
  if it is raining however
  continue on to the place
  where your chewing gum loses its flavor
  double back there...
  in a drainage ditch on your right
  you will see a sweet-faced cat
  take the first left after that
  proceeding south

112

until the sound of the pavement
changes pitch under the car
go right here
and right again at the first smell of wisteria
we're the second house
after the third speed bump
if you come to the ocean
you will know you have gone too far"

of course this was before
the advent of consciousness raising
and assertiveness training...
nowadays
when a guest is late to arrive
it's the female standing at the gate
anxiously inquiring
if the directions were all right
while the house husband
comes bumping
backward through the kitchen door
all smiles
hoping you enjoyed the drive

Shopping for Clothes
by Gender

much
of what makes up my wardrobe
began as a gift...
an unpleasant birthday
or Christmas surprise
shirts and ties
i would never have bought for myself
but in the name of thrift wore
and in wearing
developed a great fondness for
and when such an article of clothing dies
a man grieves
thereafter standing briefly
in the doorway of haberdasheries
eyes sweeping rack and shelf
and if nothing there looks familiar
leaves before a clerk can say
"may i be of help?"

in this way
i can do an entire shopping center
in about the time it takes to walk through it

on the flip side of this
my wife
picks out everything she wears
but wears nothing out
too fickle for that
her relationship with apparel
is more of a fling

a short-lived affair
good for a couple of dates
then snubbed and dismissed as
"that old thing"

entering a boutique
the woman is always on the make
unwilling to leave
until she has danced with every rag on the rack...
taking them all for a spin in the mirror
a patrotic fashion plate
she seems determined to spend eternity
on parade
wrapping herself in flags

put on hold
aimlessly wandering the mall
i stop at the window display
of a cutlery shop
and while counting the blades
on a Swiss Army knife
come up with an axiom
sharp enough to almost hold true

"when
  shopping for clothes
  men
  look for old friends
  women for new"

Obstetrics at the Rialto

*(Written after actually being there to witness the birth of my
first granddaughter Cara Masten Di Girolamo.)*

"pickles and ice cream?" he gulped
swallowing his gum
the moviegoer limp with laughter
at the dimp he'd suddenly become

i cut my eyeteeth
on these celluloid cliches...
on Hollywood tough-guys
unraveling at the first contraction
helplessly stumbling around
fumbling with the car keys...
the inevitable motorcycle cop
out from behind a billboard
to stop the wild reckless ride to the hospital
then suddenly goggle-eyed
hopping back on his machine
shouting "follow me!"

and fathers-to-be
unshaven and forlorn
sweating it out in the maternity ward hall...
chain smoking nail biters
their misery and discomfort winked at
by nurses who knew after all
that by comparison
men will never know real pain
the birthing scene itself
staged not to offend
and therefore indistinguishable
from all other screened medical events

116

everyone not directly involved
out in the kitchen boiling water
while the camera focuses discreetly
on the doctor's troubled face
as he bends above the thrashing patient
to deliver a baby
sever a leg
the sequences were interchangeable

and in the end
if the hero wasn't left
in a train station leaning on a cane
he'll be pictured passing out cigars
to the back-slapping crowd
at the observation window
proud papas
making "goo-goo" noises...
faces pressed against the glass
a school of goofy goldfish
that never failed to leave us with a laugh

from start to finish
the birthing process
emasculated by the movie version
and not knowing what else to do
John Q. Public and i
imitated art

A Largely Inherited
and Unalterable Tendency
to Desire Silence

in sand
on pine needles
a man can keep his vow of silence
but not in a modern convenience
flooded to the rim
with no shoreline
to go upon in quiet meditation

how humiliating!
to stand before God
and everyone else within earshot
announcing one's imperfection

acoustically
giving our position away
spooking the game
putting the enemy on alert
instinctual no-no's i'd say

and yet like a wolf
trotting from house to house
the civilized male is obliged
to mark off his territory
in disinfected pails of water

is it any wonder then
that modern men these days
under pressure
are melting into the shadows
and losing themselves in the trees

118

A Norman King

middle-aged and bored beyond belief
i went into the brush today
and like a child made myself a clearing

with grub hoe and axe
i fought the undergrowth
and did battle
with the greasewood and genista...
the going wasn't easy
the bushes striking – slashing back
until the branches brought me crashing down
a whip-like blow across the face

"thanks
  i needed that"

then cursing in childish rage
i rise a Norman king to chop and hack
at the very root of my lethargy
take that!
and that! and that!... and

slowly – grudgingly
the enemy falls back
until at last
i have myself a piece of open ground
to rest on...
to lie upon and watch the sky from

listen the wind is cheering

heavy things
in hard places

Anatomy of a Zealot

"machines
  have been devised
  to accurately measure the age
  of found objects
  so what we have here
  has got to be the remains
  of Noah's Ark
  never mind the bones of dinosaurs
  they were cleverly put here
  to test our faith"

in matters religious
one reaches the truth
only
through good hard
investigative thought
however when one
is thoroughly convinced
that the truth is found
it then
becomes necessary
to stop thinking

The Denny's Menu

"a toasted English muffin
 with whipped creamy butter
 and a steaming mug
 of mountain-grown coffee"
it all sounds so good on the menu

"fresh ranch eggs"
conjuring up pictures
of mother father and me on an outing...
flying through a summer countryside
in an open Tin Lizzy
mother holding her floppy hat in the wind
laughing...
banjo music playing
and chickens everywhere!
scattering...
scurrying back to a barn
full of sunshine cracks and aromatic shadows
where clucking hens
nest in secret places
laying eggs for children to find
put into baskets and bring us for breakfast

yeah!
i'll have some of that this morning

pretending
i've not been to the concentration camp
and seen the eyes staring through the wire
and seen the miles and miles

124

of shopping-basket cells
with barely room enough to move or sleep
forgetting
how they helplessly stand for days
eating off tin trays
drinking from galvanized tanks
watching their life's work roll away like teeth

taken out of the circle of things
"crispy bacon strips and country-cured ham"
have nothing to do with the slaughter

we eat words
and no one says grace
and no one gives thanks

A Sneaking Suspicion

i have given my pets the power
and let my little dog Amazing Grace
get such a grip on me
that more than once i've folded maps
and called off an extended trip
it becoming more than i can bear
to watch her napping in the sun so unaware
trusting to the moment
oblivious to the desire of man and flea

the side of me that lags behind and drags its feet
gets hold of my imagination
till i have myself confined
in the wire world of the kennel
waiting in canine limbo brave and stoic
with pricked ears listening
keeping watch on the door
expecting each moment to be the moment
the Master reappears

and i do this to myself
till i must cancel travel plans
deciding not to go
unable to stand the thought of missing myself so

that
and the sneaking suspicion
that once on the road i'll forget her
as quickly as i will be replaced
by something
alive and moving in the brush

126

With a Pierced Ear

sitting on United – flight 394
with a pierced ear
i find i have velocity and direction

where i have come from i'm not quite sure
where i am going i do not care

the ticket says Philadelphia
i'm not there though
i only know i am somewhere
filled with this feeling
and aware of it

strange
how i keep leaving behind
the very thing it is that i am reaching for
but then life is for living
time is a spiral
and every road
the road home

look for me
i'm coming

Before Mr. Howard
Comes Along, Mrs. James

let me say
i have done this long enough to know
i don't write my poems
we do
and so i live much like
that indistinct little man in
western movies
the one in shirt-sleeves and vest
who seems to exist only at the window
of the telegraph office
never shot – never kissed
his reason for being
simply a gimmick to further the plot

like him i sit at the end of my pen
hunched over sending and receiving
taking the messages down
reading them back to you
and this just came over the wire:

GOOD NEWS STOP EVERY HUMAN RELA-
TIONSHIP THAT HAS EVER BEEN OR WILL
EVER BE ENDS STOP GOOD NEWS ONLY IF
WE USE THE INFORMATION AND TELL THE
PEOPLE WE LOVE THAT WE LOVE THEM
AND DO IT TODAY STOP TOMORROW IS
ONLY A FIGMENT OF OUR IMAGINATION
STOP

       I LOVE YOU
           JESSE

128

Without Kite and Key

i can understand the stove
the bifocal
and some of the other stuff
but Benny
without the kite and the key
what in hell is electricity?

and please spare me
the zero/infinity form of energy routine
seeming to this untutored mind
a kind of doctrinal line
demanding a greater leap of faith
than a Catholic or Baptist makes

it strikes me ...
(a little electrical-engineering humor there)
that you who believe in electricity
should wear a habit and shave your head
to go with the mystical smile that you smile
while seeing the light
pretending you know what goes on

you may be pious enough
to actually own a Phillips screwdriver
one of the chosen few but where is the juice
when the generator shuts down?

like the spirit and soul of the dear departed
where has it gone?

Remembering Alan Watts

i've been told
that the church won't saint a man
until he's been dead at least fifty years
and that's too bad
for who will be around then
to tell us how he talked too much
and used to pick his nose

let me tell about a saint of mine
who
not so long ago
was alive and well and living in California

i had read every word he had written
and could recite his punch lines
like the rosary...
he was only a writer of books then though

he became a saint the night we met
and he was drunk
and fell on the floor vomiting
and...

set me free

A Philosopher
(for Bob O'Brian)

an honest-to-god philosopher
lives in the mountains close to me
farther up though and much further out

he is
the department at a local community college
eighty miles round trip each day
he goes the distance for questions

twice now
he has summoned me personally
to help him with a problem
he couldn't handle by himself

1. a twenty-four-foot house trailer
down a sixty-percent slope
we almost lost it on the dogleg left

2. a ton of machinery
over a precipice on a frayed rope
was the only way to get the pump to water

twice now
we have seen the strawberry
growing on the face of the cliff
twice now
we have almost eaten it
it would seem then
that a philosopher by definition
is someone who has dedicated his life
to putting heavy things in hard places

The Writing on the Wall

if we show them at all
most of us who write our secrets down
and call it poetry
prefer to slip it under the door and run
and if we must be present at the reading
disguise ourselves
in sotto voce and pale monotone

but here was one
who could take us into his personal life
and show us around
as if it were a house for sale
exposing everything the way it was
and never once it seemed rushing ahead
to straighten up a room or kick the dirty linen
underneath a bed

i got my questions ready...
how could he do it? – and why?
it was such private property
and we were total strangers
just in off the street – looking
not necessarily there to buy
but then toward the end of the tour
i realized that there was nothing in this place
i hadn't seen before
and when i told him this at the door
he took me by the hand
and thanked me
for helping him feel so at home

outside as we were leaving
i saw where some street philosopher
had taken paint
and sprayed a classic on the wall

there are no strangers here – it read
i know myself
therefore
i know you all

On the Mountain

somewhere about a third of the way up
he came striding down the trail
and caught me unaware
a poet
staff in hand – naked – thin as a whip
wild gray hair framing the sun-stained face
his bright eyes blue holes
the sky showing through

when he saw me resting there
he laughed out loud – "friend" he said
"i have been to the summit
  and found nothing there – absolutely nothing"
then laughing again
he went on down around the bend
and left me

with my brand-new dayglow knapsack
ten dollar compass – waterproof boots
remembering how i'd sharpened my knife
till it shaved the hair on the back of my wrist
preparing myself for almost anything
but this

still i was young then
and it wasn't until i too
had run out of places to climb
that i began to wonder
where he was going and what he was after
laughing that way

so i turned around
and followed on down behind
and if i took you by surprise
this morning coming down the path
believe me
i was only laughing at myself
sitting there

A Troubadour
and Traveling Salesman

at home
my heart is a wristwatch
and there is always a dog
in the calendar

suddenly i am a rabbit
breaking cover
my ears up in the wind
i go sailing

the mountains
drain from my window
underfoot the floor moves
the waiting is over

outward bound
we clear the harbor
like farmers
coming in from the field

On Butterfly Wings

you know for the life of me
i can't recall what happened last Good Friday...
Christmas i can
because mother got smashed
and the baby seeing his image distorted
on the surface of a thousand ornaments
cried all day
and on Easter it rained
so that the candy hidden in the grass got sticky
and we had to wash the ants off
before we let the kids out
but somehow i missed Good Friday

looking the other way i guess
like i do
when i pass someone walking the roadside
with an empty gas can
muttering under my breath
about the high cost of funerals
and how the undertakers are bleeding us dry
like vampires
not stopping to realize
that we can't pay those guys enough
to handle what scares us half to death

i mean
if Aunt Maude bites the bag in my kitchen
you're gonna find me outside in the yard
waiting for some weird cat
to roll up

in a long black vehicle
and clean up the mess – cart the problem away
smiling all the while
oh
i'll stop by the parlor Saturday afternoon...
check the flowers out
and have a quick look in the box
but then i never was able to accept a gift graciously
and it's my loss
and no doubt the reason
i sit in my own small house drinking coffee
feeling homesick most of the time

an old guru once told me
that the only thing
we really have to do in this life
is die
and i think i shall repeat this statement
over and over...
a hundred times each night
before i go to sleep

perhaps
if i could bring myself to believe it
i mean really believe it
and remember what happens on Good Friday
i just might come out and find myself
some sunny Easter morning
on butterfly wings
rising!

138

Looking for Patterns

i collect small
typewritten words
and fly them
looking for patterns

sometimes they rise from me
in clouds
like birds off a field
to circle and then wheel away
for no apparent reason
and i
lie empty as a pasture
left behind
defined only by these dark fences
of mine

western civilization
waiting for the punch line

missing the point

**the walt whitman
extension**

A BIT ABOUT
THE WALT WHITMAN EXTENSION

One of the many wonderful traits Walt Whitman had was that he kept dressing his old poems in new clothes — rewriting, re-editing, and republishing them in new forms — so that one can have a shelf of Whitman's books which are more or less the same book over and over, each with a few new poems added to the revamped old ones. And what's wrong with that? For what am I but the same person I was a few weeks, months and years ago, slightly rewritten and re-edited? And if things have gone well, I have added a few brand new thoughts to those already in my head. I can't do a complete makeover on myself every time I go out — I do, however, enjoy re-evaluating and re-affirming my best old ideas and feelings and folding new ones into the mix.

This is what Ric is doing with this book. He has shown us, in the poems he has written, his understanding of the world he has traveled through, and even now he has not stopped on that road — there are new vistas and points of view from where he finds himself now along with the old ones from where he has been. And more new ones just around the corner.

His poetry is in a sense his sculpture, the art of which, Michelangelo said, consisted not so much in creating the work out of a block of marble as in chipping away the parts that don't belong. So here is Ric with a few more pieces chipped away, the whole sculpture emerging slowly with each new poem but

143

still dependent on all the work that has gone before. Read the new ones in the light of the old and the old in the light of the new — they'll take on slightly different hues.

I've struggled to present some subtle and thoughtful new sides to Ric, not to mention Whitman and Michelangelo, but the problem with writing about talented people is that they can do with a few strokes of their pens and chisels what I can't do even with many strokes of mine. However, since I was the one who wrote the introduction to this book's first version, and now am writing the follow-up for this new section, everything I've said of these people reinventing themselves and their art can be said of me, and maybe I'm really creating a mighty ... Ah, Jim, don't get fancy — just tell 'em to enjoy the poems.

Jim Parkman
Hermosa Beach, California

The Challenge

(For Francisco X. Alarcón,
a poet of enormous talent and girth;
brimming with mesoamerican wisdom —
Latin American mirth.

And for Javier,
a delightfully shy young man
with limited English
but a handsome piñata
full of sweet surprises.)

*****

the Pacific
was particularly playful that day
racing back and forth
tickling our feet
sneaking up behind to splash us
in the seat of the pants
then dancing away
giggling

at the base of the cliff
where the sand ends
there is a natural granite bridge
if you stand at just the right place
the horizon winks at you
through the opening

"What shall we call it?"
Francisco challenges

"I will call it: ¡La Puerta al Mar!
 The Doorway to the Sea!"
the 1993
National Book Award winner
dares me to be as creative

what a pregnant occasion!
what a rare opportunity
to raise
the level of my poetic stock
but phrases like "Punctured Stone"
and "Neptune's Peephole" elude me
after a long ponderous moment
all i can think of is:
"¡Rock with a Hole in it!"

a week later
retracing our footprints
i still wallow
in waves of laughter

An Exercise
in Self-Depreciation

i am dazzled
by your incredible command
of the English language....

your extraordinary use of syntax
and lyrical elegance
makes it impossible
for me to imagine you
ordering pizza
or changing a typewriter ribbon

dampened
by your most recent
published poetic triumph
i sit numbly at my writing desk
playing basketball with the waste-bin
glumly wishing it were possible
to go head to head with you
one on one
in a winner take all
belching contest

Storm in a Nutshell

a retired
brigadier general
joins the anchor man
at the CNN news desk
he is there to describe the latest
in US high-tech hardware...
matter-of-fact at first
almost bored
but when the M1A1 Abrams
plowed across the screen
he caught his breath
warming to the task
his voice taking on an excited
George C. Scott rasp
 "i'm a tanker myself
 and what
 you're looking at now
 is ninety tons of rolling death!"

from here
we switched over
and watched the Green Bay Packers
kick the living daylights
out of some
hick town high school team
getting all teary-eyed
when the fans stood up
and sang the national anthem

A Clean Well-Kept
Wild Animal Zoo

perched
above counterfeit logs
and troweled rocks
owls appear stuffed
and if the coyote paced
like a shooting gallery target
and the crows bitched at the grated sky
still
it was evident that the beaver pond
was chlorinated
and the paper under the fox
religiously replaced
from fence to fence
the compound carefully raked
to resemble the surface of water
elk and mule-deer
tracking up the effect
"do not tease
 or mistreat the animals"
the irony
was posted everywhere

at the exit
a slotted glass box
expected our goodwill
but all the Park
and Recreation Department
got from me was this
and a meticulously folded
three-dollar bill

149

Two Guys in a Pickup Truck
for Fred Hernandez

over Chinese
telling my good friend Fred Hernandez
about the break-in robberies
occurring in our neck of the woods
i mentioned that a couple of Latinos
(a liberal always uses
the current accepted ethnic term)
were seen that day
cruising the neighborhood
in a pickup truck

to which Fred launched into
this seemingly off-the-wall story
about an acquaintance of his
once saying to his face
that Mexicans were a lazy lot

"in case you hadn't noticed"
Fred responded
"my name is Hernandez"

"hey — don't get me wrong"
the man says
"i wasn't talking about you"

and to think i had
turned in to my own driveway
before realizing
that i should have described
our suspected perpetrators

150

simply as two suspicious looking guys
seen that day in a pickup truck

phrased that way
however
we would have missed the fun
of seeing another bleeding-heart liberal
being shot down by a prejudiced remark
that had obviously
been parked down there for years
in a blind spot

Reading the Road Signs

gridlocked — gripping the steering wheel
inching forward in fits and starts
i wonder about the trouble ahead....
a well-known pessimist once said
that like a snowball
rolling toward the lip of a ledge
America's problems have grown
so enormous that what little we could do
to change direction would simply not be enough
to keep us from going over the edge

i'd like to say i don't agree
but stalled here on the freeway
watching opportunist after opportunist
pull out and speed away
using the shoulder illegally
the law breakers
too numerous now to be arrested
they know the CHP will only merge them back in
near the head of the line
a thousand cars better off than before
and seeing this i realize
that these are the kind of people
who succeed in business

yesssss!
you can almost hear them hiss
pumping a fist
slapping the dash in victory
back up to speed we head for the crash

152

Coming of Age in America

a driver's license?
the first legal drink? — casting a vote?
i am afraid these contemporary milestones
pale beside the purity
of the white-faced aborigine's walkabout
or the way an African youth goes off alone
to chase a lion down — here in America without
such clear-cut transformation experiences
it is difficult to escape the jail
of perpetual adolescence

looking for my own
personal moment of changeover
i discover that i was almost forty
the night my mother peeked into the icebox
eyed the vandalized turkey ruins and shrieked
"all right! who stole the Pope's nose?"
the poor distraught woman
anguishing over her stolen treat —
her missing midnight snack —
collapsing like a Kurdish widow
against the refrigerator door while i
slipped out the back way and headed home
changed forevermore

my coming-of-age ordeal — my lion
my bridge out of immaturity
would have to be the blinding realization
that what is in my parent's fridge
does not belong to me

Oratorus Rex!
*(The Feminization
of the Department of Ministry)*

not long ago these grand grey-maned gargantuans
ruled the theological plain
Oratorus Rex!
the rest of us jumping up and down
like toy poodles at the neck of great danes
but in the mucky discourse
that followed dinner last night
the dinosaur came to the end of its reign

there
mired in a tar pit of yesterday's thinking
unable to free themselves
from too much Chardonnay
they bellowed and raged — thrashing about
sawing the charged air with their teeth
bewildered — wounded — feeling betrayed
no longer able to throw their weight around
they went down slowly glaring directly into our eyes

today their reputation is all that remains
left like petrified footprints
to be measured and intellectualized
by smaller more maneuverable creatures
unable to fully comprehend
the enormous size
and majesty these giants once had

there is always something about
a change for the better that is terribly
terribly sad

154

A Loaded Shopping Cart

"wha'cha doing Ann?"
this to a woman
pushing a loaded shopping cart
in the Safeway parking lot

"stocking up for the weekend"
she'll say
or
"my folks are here from the East"
or
"tomorrow is Alex's birthday"

"wha'cha doing Dan?"
question a man
doing the same thing
and you get

"completing my Ph.D."
or
"i'm still with Village Electric"
or
"working for Merrill Lynch again"

"wha'cha doing?"
ask her
ask him
and listen to the difference
between women and men

Life-Long Companions

like old shoes...
that comfortable
that familiar
that everyday
and we swore to never let it get
that way for us again
back then broken in and broken down
were synonymous

pinched into a tight new pair
of sexy lizard-skin boots
we were constantly reminded
that nothing can be taken for granted
passion thrives on the acute awareness
that comes with Cuban heels
and flashy patent leather
and there for a time we did dance on the edge
in our trendy wooden clogs
certain that an old-shoe relationship
would be one that had gone to the dogs

but after forty plus years in close proximity
i've found that the dogs
is not all that bad a place to be
you and me together
like two friendly old hounds
out on the lawn fondly
gnawing on one another

...like old shoes

Opportunity
of a Lifetime

out walking one day
an elderly fellow
was greatly surprised
when from a puddle
beside the road
he heard a toad frog say

"kiss me
and I'll turn into a gorgeous blond
with whom you can have
your mad impetuous way"

and scooping up
the flirtatious amphibian
he stuffed it securely
into the deep pocket
of his overcoat

"hey!"
came a muffled cry
"i said if you kiss me
i'll turn into a gorgeous blond
with whom you can have
your mad impetuous way"

but the old boy
kept right on walking
down the road
"at my age" he said
"i'd rather have a talking toad"

Crunching the Numbers

i hadn't seen the woman
since her daughter's wedding
"how are the newlyweds getting on?"
i gushed as if proposing a toast
"divorced two years"
she said
devastated i steadied myself
"that didn't last long
 what has it been?
 four years? — five at the most?"

"try fifteen"

"impossible!" i protested
blind-sided by the disturbing figure
the two of us huddling together
grimly crunching the numbers

a disheartening exercise
the young will never comprehend
after all fifteen years is a lifetime
to a fifteen-year-old
and even folks in the middle ages
are not put off
by this form of advanced math
why should they be?
when 66 take away 15
leaves a young and vital 51

but from where i am on the path
the sum of these two figures
is depressing dark and weighty
for i have either shuffled off
or i am over eighty

158

The Obituaries
and Other Perks that Come Along with Aging

until recently
it was as if they didn't exist...
if i thought about them at all
i thought that the people
who do read them must be masochists
then one morning i began to wonder why
we put the decorations away
what with Christmas
coming along every other day
and suddenly
the obituary column
becomes the most fascinating thing
William Randolph Hearst has to say

true
the writing is dry and humorless
the vocabulary limited
"died" being the only verb
convention and propriety allow

Gertrude Soinso, 87, of Pacific Grove
died Sunday
of complications following a stroke

and yet somehow you just know
the journalist who wrote that
was fighting back the temptation
to use the word "croaked"
but then it stands to reason
bankers should cash in

hotel managers check out
football players pass away
in the end don't you think a ballet dancer
would want to go toes up?
and contrary to popular belief
reading an obituary
is not necessarily a downer

David A. Youngman, 19, of Seaside,
died Monday
as the result of a motorcycle accident

notice of such an untimely young death
isn't sad so much as it is
a daily reminder for seniors like myself
to be grateful for all the dumb luck
and narrow escapes we've had

Thomas O. Geezer, 103, of Carmel
died Saturday of heart failure
on the 17th tee at Pebble Beach

to me the passing of some spry old duck like this
is not in the least bit depressing
it's proof positive that i — god willing
still have forty or so more to go

and best of all
if the deceased is a world-famous celebrity
someone who made it big
who captured the dream everyone else only chases
i simply regard the loss
as one less talented success
with whom i'd willingly trade places

160

Old Fossils
Carbon Dated

away from the blunt honesty
of the calendar
i am in my early thirties
most folks
sixty five or older are

however
we quickly discover
what floor we are actually at
when the furniture
that furnishes our habitat
is no longer: "how fashionable!
 how totally now!"
 but rather: "wow!
 i'll bet there's a story
 that comes with that!"

Ode to a Removable
Partial Denture
for Robert G. Morris, DDS

feigning nonchalance
like an adolescent
purchasing a prophylactic
i furtively
bought a tube of Fixodent today

a disturbing experience
although i am no stranger to the realm
of crowns bridges and caps...
remove the fixed frontal facades
and i'm left with nothing
but pegs notches and gaps
the sunny smile you see
is not the one i displayed in youth
but once the dentist's artistry
is cemented down
and the tongue wearies of exploration
one tends to forget the truth

receding hairline
tri-focals — liver spots
all have been taken in stride
but not this recent oral acquisition
this sculpted wire amalgam
barbed and hooked where it bends
pink cocktail olives
stuffed with ivory pimentos
skewered at both ends

in place it magically fits in

but on the counter top — in the sink
it appears sinister
like some gleaming surgical device
left here
by intruders from outer space
perhaps an instrument of torture
dating from the Inquisition
my natural exuberance
curbed
by this cruel Spanish bit

and to think
for the rest of my life
i must play host
to this illusive parasite
this spiny-finned pilot fish
watching it
dart in and out of my mouth
knowing that
it is secretly holed up
somewhere in there
waiting to eat

and although
it does feel good
to dine with molars again
symbolically
the moment this metallic interloper
was parked in my mouth
marked for me
the beginning of the end

Pharaoh and the Man
from La Mancha

recently
i have lost two friends
David
the young one
succumbing to suicide
and Chuck
in his late sixties
losing a long
and grueling battle with cancer
the irony is obvious

here we have David
not quite forty
everything going for him
and opting out
the determined victim
of a bout with melancholy
unwilling
to face even one more day
David
frozen in lifeless repose
reclining on his king-size motel bed
another in the sad procession
of young dead Pharaohs

and then Chuck
grayed and grizzled
a man from La Mancha
painfully forcing himself to rise
each morning from his sick-bed

164

and tilt with extinction
Chuck
ferociously clinging to breath
wringing it out for every
precious moment he could get
stubbornly doing this
until
unhorsed at last
he reluctantly faded

Chuck and David
David and Chuck
in death —
such diverse cases
if only they had met in life
and traded places

Like Harry / Like Howard

like Harry
i don't want to blow my death
i don't want to see
a lifetime of pluck and courage
rubbed out by five weeks
of whiny fractious behavior
granted
Harry's was a scary way to go
from diagnosis to last breath
the cancer moving fast
but five weeks
of bitching and moaning
was more than enough
to erase every trace of a man
i have wanted to emulate
his wife sending word
that even she can't remember
what he was like
before his undignified departure
no —
i don't want to go out like Harry

like Howard
let me come swimming up
out of the deepening coma
face serene as if seen
through undisturbed water
breaking the surface
to eagerly take the hand
of bedside well-wishers

unexpected behavior
i must admit
as Howard has always been
a world-class hypochondriac
second only to me
the two of us able to sit for hours
discussing
the subtle shade of a mole
turning each other on
with long
drawn-out organ recitals

in the end
one would have thought
such a legendary
self-centered soul would cower
and fold up completely
like Harry
but no —
when my time comes
let me go sweetly
like Howard

Letting Go of Joe

"hefting the heavy ceramic jar
the mortician's apprentice handed it over:
'he certainly was a big fella wasn't he?'
i mean can you imagine
anyone being that insensitive
to a widow of only four days?"

Helen described the dreadful ordeal
as she lovingly lifted Joe from the car floor
"but that was nine months ago
and i've done the grief work
god knows i've done that and i think
i'm ready now to let him go"

in single file we followed Bixby creek
to the place of Joe's choosing
wife and first wife — son and stepsons
their girl friends — my family and i
keeping pace with our memories

roommates at boarding school
our friendship
didn't seep away after graduation
it deepened
Joe becoming my zen friend and teacher
the two of us always joking about death
playing with the existential fear
laughing at the mere thought of ending up
in a hermetically sealed
upholstered box

168

a stiff grinning leather effigy
all spiffied up
in an elegant smoking jacket
how Egyptian
we would laughingly agree

but that was then
and this was the sandy shore
below Bixby bridge
where we would sit a spell in a close circle
listening to the roar of the Pacific
underscore our words of farewell

after which
and i want to get this part right
there is the sight of Helen
knee-deep in the boiling surf
denim pant legs darkening
kelly green sweater damp
bent over slightly
one hand tightly clutching Joe to her heart
the other cramped at the mouth of the jar
a thin figure
staggering helplessly against the tide
"Joe... i don't know how to do this!"
she cried
"help me somebody"

which we did
all of us wading in
to take a small measures of Joe in hand
grip loosening slowly
the granules sifting through our fingers
drifting into the foaming wash

onto the coarse wet sand
doing this repeatedly
strangely comforted at how easily
one becomes part of the beach
part of the whole again
from start to finish Joe never could
pass up an opportunity to teach

as for Helen
i knew she'd be all right when
involved in this activity
for more than a little while
i was surprised to find that the urn
was still nearly half full
and looking up at me
cheeks streaked and glistening with tears
she smiled broadly
"he certainly was a big fella wasn't he?"

Sow Bugs

as screwed up
as the father of the Prodigal Son
i overlook my three success stories
and focus on the one going sour
hour upon hour of self-flagellation
working myself over with "what ifs"
"i should have's" and "why didn't i's"

Reed Farrington
my philosophic friend declares
that he thinks the way kids turn out
is a completely random affair
pick up a rock and watch the sow bugs
scramble in every direction
bugs onto the sidewalk stepped on and squished
bugs into the pond dined on by fish
bugs running blindly find the right spot
having nothing to do with the way
the bugs were brought up
in this world some bugs make it
and some do not

however
as a long-suffering parent
yearning for Prince Charming to replace Mr. Scuzz
i tell my friend that i'm holding out
for a minor miracle
to which he responds:
"remember the bugs that made it to safety?
 well what do you think that was?"

They're Back!

"writer's block" by my definition
is a poet with an empty bag of woe
of late a condition i need not fear
because every other year
like the sequel
of a hit horror movie
"they're back!"

this time the addicted are evicted
once again dumping
their offspring on us
the prodigal son
and his female accomplice on the run
using a hard-luck story like a gun
to fleece family and friends
"food for the boys" they lie
using the ill-gotten goodwill
to feed a habit they both deny

if you know my work
this probably sounds redundant
but looking at life sideways as i do
a circle is really a spiral
and this time around we are truly
all in a different place
the boys older— a little more damaged
certainly more unruly
my tolerance of wet beds
loud music and bad movies
less than before

172

add to this the burden
of knowing that when
the constant infighting is under control
and the situation normalizes
the phone will ring and everything
is right back out the door

and having explored
the subject at some length
i know the addict
must hit rock bottom before Detox
and Rehab look like programs
they might want to enter
and to that end i also know
that taking the kids in
doesn't help a bit but buzz words
like "enable" and "co-dependence"
are claptrap to a petrified grandparent
watching the horror
forced to sit front row center

chilled to the bone
unable to close my eyes
i wish it would hurry up
and be over
and we all could go home

Support System

in the driveway
of a renovated apartment complex
dwarfing a chair
the continent of Africa sat
getting a haircut
the barber — a Latina
wore soiled institutional whites
i slowed to first gear
"i'm looking for Genesis House" i said
and the haircut said: "you're here
 visitors register over there"

i followed the motion of his head
to a doorway marked "Office"
a group of marginal-looking people
stood around it — chain smoking
eyeing me suspiciously
one of them approached
"hi Dad
 i didn't think anyone would come"

and why should he
considering all the years
of lies manipulation and denial
"neither did i" i said signing in

after that it was a minefield
father and son taking up positions
at opposite ends of a dusty old couch
that sat outside in the yard

174

gingerly stepping around
the dangerous ground
avoiding the obvious trip wires
sticking to safe subjects
i held my tongue
determined not to set him off
or blow up myself

perhaps later in the recovery
we can sweep the relationship clean
digging up and disarming the booby traps
but for now
to survive the war for even a short visit
was more than enough

getting up to go
i told him about how much we enjoy
taking care of his son Little Ricky
and about waiting
at the mailboxes each day
to meet the car pool
sadly adding the grim footnote
that when he was a boy
coming home from school
i can't remember... ever...
doing as much for him

"well you did today Dad"

as i left i looked back
and was surprised to see the haircut
and some of the other residents
waving
as if i were family

Bag of Woe Fable

during my readings
there are always moments
when i can almost hear
the audience asking:
how can you use that
as grist for your poetry mill?
how can you dwell
on such private property
at least with out masking
the details?
well —
for the feedback of course
the war stories
that my stories prompt you to tell
but perhaps
the question is best answered
in the "bag of woe" fable

the "once upon a time" tale
about the troubled village of Contrary
its harried citizens
and the magical mystical miracle worker
who showed up one dreary day
saying: "i am aware
 of your torment and woe
 and i am here to lighten your load!"

he then
instructed the beleaguered citizens
to go home

176

and rummage through their harried lives
"bag up your troubles" he said
"both large and small
 stuff them all in a sack
 and drag them down to the town square
 and stack them around on the wall"

and when everyone was back
and every bag was there
the magical mystical miracle worker said:
"it's true — just as i promised
 you won't have to take
 your sack of troubles home
 leave it behind when you go
 however you will have to take along
 somebody's bag of woe"

so
the citizens of Contrary
all went to find their own bag
and shouldering the load discovered
that it was magically and mystically
much easier to carry

Coach Bill
MUSTANG LEAGUE — 9 and 10 year olds

David!
strike one
don't just stand there!
strike two
praying for a walk!
strike three...oh me!

strike one
Andrew!
strike two
don't swing at everything
strike three
that goes by...oh my!

Jack!
strike one
be a hitter big guy...*crack!*
now we're having fun!
only next time Jack
remember to run

settle down pitcher
play catch with the catcher
just hit the mitt
you can do it Ray!
...oh well that's okay

pop up — easy out
get under it Paul

178

let go of the mask Paul!
don't freeze...oh jeez!

remember Joey
the play is at home plate
not first base
do not throw to first base!
no! no! ...oh no!

pay attention outfield
the game is over here
on your feet Wally!
be aware!
what is happening out there?!

Ricky stand still!
stop dancing around
you don't have to pee
do you? ...oh gee!

two outs bases loaded
get this guy and we win
you can do it gang ...oh dang!

circle up team!
2 - 4 - 6 - 8
who do we appreciate?
Bluebird Freight & Storage! ...yea

next week Ace Tool & Dye
best record in the league
of course we'll win
see you then
...*sigh!*

Dixieland Jazz Festival
or the Longest Afternoon in History

i recently
spent a week one afternoon
in Dixieland
outnumbered and overrun by hordes
of latter-day flappers with lavender hair
and paunchy old guys in white Panama suits
truckin' on down
one finger waving in the air
my reaction summed up
in the wince and pained look
on the face of a kid
in the local high school jazz band
the one on alto who could really cook —
standing next to Nathan
my grandson who
as you might guess
was the only reason i was there

the first hour
passed pleasantly enough
though i did wish Nathan
had been asked
to do more than just play backup
the caste system of high school i judged
Nathan being but a mere freshman
it was during the lengthy wait
for the kids to perform again
where time refused to budge
Nathan abandoning me
"to enjoy the rest of the Festival"

180

understandably
preferring to "hang with his friends"

and so
for forty days and forty nights
i wandered from clinic to clinic
a bored cynic pushed along
by crowds of loud aficionados
wondering what ever became
of the Dixieland fan i used to be
the foot stomping collegiate
who drove to San Francisco
twice a week
to dig the beat of Turk Murphy
long gone it seems
my taste in music having relocated
to a cooler less intrusive place

yet there i was mired
in this unremitting ragtime morass
feeling tired — lethargic
on the verge of snoring
torturing myself
i stayed awake
by making connections
between being bored and being boring
between wishing time would pass
and suicide

then abruptly
i heard the trombone player shout
"take it Nathan!"
to which my grandson
stood and belted out his first solo ever

concluding
with such a shy self-conscious smile
it made
the longest afternoon in history
all worthwhile

i suppose
such fluctuations in the time frame
seem routine
to those of you going through
the Little League
and dance recital years
but not for me
who in a former life
missed every game and concert
pursuing my career

Pebbles and Crumbs

last summer
whenever possible
my visiting granddaughter Cara
would worm her tiny hand into mine
and like Hansel and Gretel
we'd strike out from the house —
up the "barking dog"trail
to the "creaky swings"
don't you love the labels
little children put on things?
and after a few "sky flying"
"watch me Grandpa" s
it was on to the "sneaky table"
where hidden in the shade
beneath a giant live oak tree
we would split
the forbidden can of Coke i brought
— "damn it Dad her teeth will rot!"

rested and refreshed
we then ascend the "slidey steep"
to check the water level
in the "water keep"
to lift the lid and take a peek
then down the trail in single file we go
through the "witchy woods"
all the way to Arizona
which is what
my spouse has dubbed the shack
she uses as her dream shop and studio
Grandma it seems

also has a knack for naming things
— "if anyone calls
    tell them I'm in Arizona"

next stop —
the family memorial garden
where we solemnly commune with the trees
Kim and Emil have become
chanting softly as we pass
— "from ashes to ashes
    to flowering plum"

then wending our way
along a stretch of "dusty dirt"
we search for yesterday's footprints
covering them with today's
"backward walking" sometimes
— "to fool our enemies
    and friends"

and always during the final leg
of this backyard expedition
my companion lags behind
little Miss Slowpoke
gathering specimens —
repeating after me the name
of every trailside shrub and tree
"eucalyptus — sticky monkey
 lilac — sage — madrone"
and "don't touch that it's poison oak"
then suddenly — "we're home!"

last summer
Cara and i collected

184

and polished these moments
scattering them along the path
like pebbles
to be utilized in the distant future
the way
a whiff of cigar smoke
brings my grandfather back
to poke about in the garden
with his walking stick
the way
my grandmother's face magically appears
at the taste of peppermint
her watchful presence close at hand
whenever i shake sand
from something that has been to the beach

i know
that on some faraway tomorrow
a sip of Cola on a hot day —
a pinch of sage —
the creaking sound a rope swing makes
these things with Cara's help
will bring me back to life again

and thankful as I am
for such life-extending crumbs
sadly i also know
that the cigar smoke and peppermint trick
can only be done by me —
in a couple of generations
it all becomes
a banquet for the crows

The Dismantling
of Pony Island

submerged in sadness
i acknowledge
the relentless passage of time
Pony Island is gone
and oddly
the demolition man was me

i say oddly
because from the nineteenth of July
to the twelfth of August
i watched entranced
while my visiting granddaughters
worked the fantasy out
in the dirt driveway
below my writing-room window

Cara
the solemn nine-year-old
bossing the job
with Gaia
a lively firecracker five
taken on as the tireless "go fer"
the two of them
spending the long summer afternoons
raiding the wood box
pilfering rocks from the garden walls
sneaking my tools out of the shop
digging and scraping
shaping the pliable surface
into every little girl's
enchanted sand-box dream

186

barn and stables
paddock and polo field
a steeplechase — a race track
pastures — pond and stream
all of this
surrounded by bright blue water
an equestrian Bali Ha'i
set in the center of a make-believe sea

"Pony Island!"
Cara proclaimed as Gaia
meticulously
breathlessly
endlessly
explained the intricate topography

but as previously revealed
this enchanted domain is no more
because for
reasons i have yet to understand
the moment
i returned home from the airport
i went
with shovel and rake in hand
directly to the now-abandoned
building site
and almost without thinking
strangely driven
i thoroughly policed the area
returning blocks and sticks
to the wood box
filling in ditches furrows and holes
removing the carefully placed
rocks and twigs

raking and watering
until there was nothing left

nothing
except the awful melancholy inside
at the center— like an island
and the sound of hoof beats
racing off
down a deserted beach
disappearing the way time does

The Haunting of Highway 1

Pacific Coast Highway number 1
is my conduit to and from
for a few it has become hearth and home
a bedroll under a bridge
a Visqueen lean-to

just ahead
a roadside figure trudges along
with the measured stride
and stubborn demeanor
of someone who once said
"i've never worked a day in my life
 and i never will"
endowed
with a well-healed doting mother
he doggedly kept the vow
and when she died
his portion of the family pension
kept him afloat for a while
at least until a bad investment deal
in asbestos ran him down
and left him walking
on the apron of my attention

and something about this
puts me five miles ahead
a quarter century back
when hurrying home one stormy Christmas eve
a bulldog checking out a road-kill
looked up
startled in the headlight glare

obviously well-bred — pedigreed
leather collar with silver studs
time standing still
until the sudden sickening thud
perhaps
because it was so late
because it was Christmas eve
because my children
were asleep in the rear seat
and a tree was waiting to be trimmed
because... at the time to drive on
was all that i could manage

exiting
this troubled memory
i see that we have passed
the bedragled pedestrian
previously described
and sitting beside me
i hear my son-in-law say:
"yeah, it bothers me too
 and he's only my wife's uncle.
 i can't imagine how it must feel to you"

of course
the outcome of this doesn't matter
it only matters
that twenty-five years after the fact
i stopped
and went back
to see if there was anything i could do

A Bus Ride
(for a young man on his way to being old)

if Air Stream is the make
of a vehicle of transportation
then the stream of consciousness
is the rapid transit bus
i take
     all too often
a detached commuter
slumped against the window
indifferent — bored
remembering only the breakdowns
the wreck
and a viewpoint or two
most of the trek
ignored
     but here
halfway down
the backside of my life
i force myself
to use my eyes and ears
to look at what i am seeing
listen to what i hear
and the urgency to do this
intensifies
with each passing year

what a waste it would be
to arrive at journey's end
the on-going moment
dropping us off with no idea
of how we got there
or where we've been

BOOKS

Also available on order, through local bookstores that use R. R. Bowker Company Books-in-Print catalogue system.

☐ I KNOW IT ISN'T FUNNY BUT...   paper $12.00
Revised and including the **Walt Whitman Extension**
by Ric Masten
208 pages. ISBN 0-918949-41-6

☐ RIC MASTEN SPEAKING (The Book)   paper $8.00
by Ric Masten
160 pages. Paper Mache Press   ISBN 0-918949-11-4

☐ NOTICE ME!   paper $7.00
by Ric Masten
110 pages. ISBN 0-931104-17-3

☐ EVEN AS WE SPEAK   paper $7.00
by Ric Masten
112 pages. ISBN 0-931104-12-3

☐ STARK NAKED   paper $6.00
by Ric Masten
110 pages. ISBN 0-931104-04-1

☐ VOICE OF THE HIVE   paper $6.00
by Ric Masten
104 pages. ISBN 0-931104-02-5

TAPES

☐ RIC MASTEN SPEAKING (The Tape)   cassette $9.00
Interview, Live Concert, Song
Stereo, Paper Mache   ISBN 0-918949-12-2

☐ RIC MASTEN SINGING   cassette $12.00
12 Songs Stereo, SF-1002
ISBN 0-931104-30-0

Checks made out to:
SUNFLOWER INK
37931 PALO COLORADO ROAD
CARMEL, CA 93923
                              ORDER $...............
        7 1/2% SALES TAX (CAL. RES.) $...............
              SHIPPING AND HANDLING $2.50
                              TOTAL $...............

NAME_____

ADDRESS_____

CITY_____STATE_____ZIP_____

☐ Include most recent catalogue with order.